Greek Take-Out Cookbook

Favorite Greek Takeout Recipes to Make at Home

Lina Chang

Disclaimer and Terms of Use

Effort has been made to ensure that the information in this book is accurate and complete. However, the author and the publisher do not warrant the accuracy of the information, text, and graphics contained within the book due to the rapidly changing nature of science, research, known and unknown facts, and internet. The author and the publisher do not hold any responsibility for errors, omissions, or contrary interpretation of the subject matter herein. This book is presented solely for motivational and informational purposes only.

The recipes provided in this book are for informational purposes only and are not intended to provide dietary advice. A medical practitioner should be consulted before making any changes in diet. Additionally, recipe cooking times may require adjustment depending on age and quality of appliances. Readers are strongly urged to take all precautions to ensure ingredients are fully cooked in order to avoid the dangers of foodborne illnesses. The recipes and suggestions provided in this book are solely the opinion of the author. The author and publisher do not take any responsibility for any consequences that may result due to following the instructions provided in this book.

ISBN: 978-1535578523

Printed in the United States

— THE —
COOK BOOK
PUBLISHER

Contents

Introduction

Greek cuisine is a remarkable blend of East and West. It is Mediterranean cuisine at its best with diverse influences. From the East are the touches of exotic spices, and from the West are the Italian additions of garlic and tomato. Greek dishes make use of fresh produce and what is abundant in different regions in Greece such as grains, legumes, vegetables, meat, seafood, olive oil, and rice. Wine often accompanies a meal. Greek food is not only delicious, it is has its own unique combinations of colors and flavors using healthy low fat, highly nutritious ingredients. To savor Greek cuisine is to savor history, culture, and love. Every Greek home cook prepares dishes using the freshest ingredients – thoughtfully seasoned with herbs and spices – prepared in age old tradition to preserve nutrients, for a happy and healthy family.

History

Takeout food has been in Greek culture since ancient times, dating back to the days of Pompeii, though Greek takeout in America has been modified through the years to suit the North American palate. American ingredients have been added, depending on availability. Greek salad in the US, for example, contains lettuce, which is not found in the original recipe. The traditional dishes of legumes and greens in traditional Greek homes have been replaced by unfamiliar concoctions, containing more meat and dairy.

Many dishes that are popularly known as Greek, such as *Moussaka* and *tzatsiki*, were created in the early 1900s and are actually Arabic in origin. Tomatoes are said to have been added to Greek cooking in the 1920s. And, though traditional Greek dishes involve simple cooking methods, many dishes nowadays employ French cooking techniques.

Modern Greek cooking has been highly influenced by Greek chef Nicholas Tselementes, who released his cookbook in the 1920s. Tselementes introduced many French techniques and made an effort to come up with what he perceived to be truly authentic Greek recipes. His cookbook became the bible of many Greek cooks and his recipes constitute what is considered modern Greek cooking.

Greek yogurt became popular in the late 1980s and rose in popularity in the late 1990s. This is said to be due to the (mistaken) notion that everything Mediterranean is low in fat and therefore healthier. True Greek yogurt is said to be high in fat. What is known in the US as "Greek" yogurt may actually be Bulgarian or Turkish.

Greek and other Mediterranean dishes became a trend since the early 1990s because of the fresh, simple, and low-fat ingredients. Olive oil was recognized as being better than corn or soybean oils or butter. And with its focus on fish and fresh ingredients, Mediterranean cuisine became recognized as a healthy cuisine.

Greek food is an undoubtedly flavorful experience. By cooking at home, you have a hand in choosing fresh healthful ingredients as well as cooking methods. Plus you get the satisfaction of saving money on expansive takeout meals and adapting the recipes to your own preferences.

Ingredients

Traditionally, this ancient cuisine makes use of the simplest and most basic ingredients such as grains, olive oil and wine. Here is a list of some ingredients you can expect to encounter in Greek cooking.

Dairy
The Mediterranean climate favored the raising of sheep and goats rather than cattle, and the preservation of milk through curdling – making cheese and yogurt. There are several types of Greek cheeses but the most well-known is Feta. Greek yogurt is made by straining out the whey, resulting in a thicker, more protein-rich product.

Fish and shellfish
Fish such as tuna, mullet, sardines, bass, and anchovies are frequently used as Greece is surrounded by sea.

Fruits
Instead of rich desserts which are served on special occasions, fruit such as grapes, apples, pears, and figs are usually found in Greek meals. They may be either fresh or dried.

Grains
The most popular grains in Greek cuisine are wheat and barley, often used to make breads and pasta. Rice is also used for pilafs or *dolmades* (wrapped in grape leaves).

Herbs and Spices

Popular herbs include flat-leaf parsley, dill, oregano, cilantro, thyme, mint, cumin, cinnamon, and red saffron. Dried herbs are used most of the time and are also valued for their therapeutic properties. Pepper should be freshly ground.

Legumes

Chickpeas, lima beans, split peas, and lentils are used in stews, bakes, pilafs, soups, and salads. They may be pureed to make dips.

Meat

Meat is not as frequently used in traditional Greek cuisine as it is in takeout dishes. Traditionally, meats are used on special occasions. Beef and pork are the usual meat sources while sheep and goat are used for their milk.

Nuts

Greeks love nuts, such as pine nuts, almonds, walnuts, and pistachios.

Olives

Olives are a Greek staple and have been cultivated for centuries. Brownish-black *Kalamata* olives are the most popular and are used for appetizers, stews, and salads.

Olive oil

Olive oil is has also been used since ancient times and Greek olive oil is one of the best in the world. It is usually made from the *Koroneiki* olive. Extra virgin olive oil (EVOO) is the popular form used in Greek cooking. It is the initial yield of cold pressing the olive fruit, and it is the basic fat in Greek cooking. It is also used as a dressing or dip.

Poultry

Chicken, quail, and guinea fowl are popularly used in traditional Greek cuisine.

Vegetables

Traditionally, vegetables make up a large part of Greek cuisine. Popular vegetables are zucchini, eggplant, spinach, artichokes, and tomatoes.

Wine

Wine is another staple in Greek cuisine, although it is consumed only moderately and with meals. Greek wine may be red, white, sweet, or dry. The most popular Greek alcoholic beverage is *ouzo*, an anise-flavored liqueur.

Yogurt

Greek yogurt is thicker than most other types of yogurt. It has been drained of whey so it is richer in protein and has fewer carbohydrates. It is traditionally made form goat's and sheep's milk, though modern versions are made from cow's milk. In Greek cooking, yogurt is used like a béchamel sauce for baked meats or an ingredient to make a dish tangy. It is also a condiment, a dip, or a bread spread for breakfast.

Cooking Methods

Greek cooking makes use of methods we are familiar with such as boiling, stewing, broiling or grilling, sautéing, baking, and frying. Greens in season are usually boiled. Oil, mainly olive oil, is used in varying amounts for sautéing, frying, or as an ingredient in stews, salads and most anything. Many meat dishes are stewed or slow cooked with olive oil and tomatoes. Meatballs, zucchini, potatoes, pumpkin, and even cheeses are fried in or sautéed in olive oil.

In Greek cooking, a variety of dishes using lamb, fish, potatoes, tomatoes, and other vegetables, as well as desserts are baked in shallow pans or clay pots. Meats are either charcoal-grilled or roasted.

Cooking Equipment

Anyone who has a kitchen that is well-equipped with the basic cooking utensils and equipment can cook Greek food. Here are some other helpful additions.

Food Processor
As with any cuisine, this is a useful tool. Greek recipes abound with dips and sauces that require making purees and pastes.

Graters
Greek cooking makes use of whole spices which are grated just before use, because this results in better flavor. Small graters come in handy for adding just the right amount of spices or cheese while cooking.

Metal baking pans and tins
You'll need these for baking vegetables, pies, or desserts.

Mortar and Pestle
Fresh herbs, spices, and some vegetables need to be crushed, pounded, and ground in a mortar and pestle. It is a very useful tool in Greek cooking.

Olive Oil Can
Olive oil is ubiquitous in Greek cooking. The olive oil can allows easy pouring of small quantities.

Pastry Brush
This is very usual for coating doughs, vegetables, meat, or baking dishes with oil, butter, or glazes.

Pepper Grinder
This is also very handy because Greek cooking requires freshly-ground pepper.

Saucepans
Have several of varying sizes. Greek recipes may require cooking on the stove top, of several ingredients, separately and all at once.

Steel *souvlaki* skewers
Steel is better than wood because they are reusable and more durable.

Straight Wood Rolling Pin
You can use one to apply even pressure when making Greek bread.

Whisks
For recipes that require lemon-oil mixtures, béchamel sauce, or egg mixtures.

Wooden Spoons and Spatulas
Have several in various shapes and sizes. Useful for mixing, ladling, tossing, spreading, smoothing, etc.

The recipes here will bring your favorite Greek takeout recipes into your home. Now that you've got your ingredients and equipment ready, let's start cooking!

Appetizers

Keftedakia - Greek Meatballs

Serves: 4
Preparation Time: 10 minutes
Cooking Time: 20 minutes

Ingredients
2 slices white bread, 1 inch thick
½ cup milk
3 tablespoons extra-virgin olive oil (EVOO)
1 ½ pounds ground lamb or beef
Freshly ground pepper
Kosher salt
¼ cup fresh mint, finely chopped
3 tablespoons red onion, grated
1 tablespoon fresh oregano, finely chopped
¼ teaspoon ground cinnamon
2 cloves garlic, grated or crushed to a paste

1 large egg
Juice of ½ a lemon
4 pocket-less pitas or flatbreads, cut into wedges
Tzatziki

Directions
For meatballs and pita

1. Preheat the oven to 450°F.
2. Place a cooling rack over a baking sheet or metal tray.
3. Soak the bread slices in the milk.
4. In a bowl, combine EVOO, meat, and pepper. Season with salt.
5. Mix in the mint, onions, oregano, cinnamon, crushed garlic, egg, and the lemon juice.
6. Squeeze the excess milk out of the bread and break it into pieces. Mix it into the meat mixture.
7. Form the meat mixture into balls with your hands or an ice cream scoop.
8. Place the meatballs on the cooling rack over the baking sheet and roast them in the oven for about 15 minutes, until they're cooked through.
9. Grill the pita bread until slightly browned with some dark spots (about 1 minute on each side).
10. Serve the meatballs with grilled pita bread and tzatziki.

Dolmades - Stuffed Grape Leaves

Serves: 6
Preparation Time: 30 minutes
Cooking Time: 1 hour 10 minutes

Ingredients
1 8-ounce jar grape leaves, rinsed and drained
¼ cup extra-virgin olive oil (EVOO)
1 cup chicken stock
Juice of 2 lemons

For the filling
¼ cup extra-virgin olive oil (EVOO)
1 large yellow onion, finely chopped
1 small fennel bulb, halved, cored and diced
1 teaspoon lemon zest, grated
½ cup pine nuts
1 cup long-grain rice

½ cup chicken stock
2 tablespoons dill leaves, finely chopped
¼ cup flat-leaf parsley, finely chopped
Kosher salt
Freshly ground black pepper

Directions
<u>For the filling</u>
1. Coat a large saucepan with oil and place it over medium heat.
2. Add the onion, fennel and lemon zest, and stir until soft (about 10 minutes).
3. Stir in the pine nuts and rice (about 2 minutes).
4. Add the chicken stock.
5. Reduce the heat and simmer until the rice is al dente (about 10 minutes).
6. Transfer the rice mixture into a bowl and add stir in remaining filling ingredients.
7. Set aside to cool.

<u>To prepare grape leaves</u>
8. Blanch the grape leaves in hot water for 5 minutes until pliable. Drain.
9. Remove the stems and hard veins from the leaves.
10. Pat dry with paper towels.

<u>To assemble/wrap</u>
11. Lay a grape leaf on a flat surface, shiny side down.
12. Scoop 2 tablespoons of the rice filling onto the leaf, near the stem end.

13. Fold the stem end over the filling, then fold both sides toward the middle, rolling up snugly like a cigar, but allowing a little space or looseness for rice to expand.
14. Squeeze lightly to secure the roll.
15. Repeat until there are no more leaves or filling.

Cooking the dolmades

16. Arrange the dolmades in a single layer in a large pot or Dutch oven, seam side down.
17. Pour the olive oil, broth, and the lemon juice over the dolmades. Add water, if needed, for liquid to reach halfway up the rolls.
18. Cover and simmer over low heat for 30 to 40 minutes. Dolmades should be tender when pierced with a fork.

Saganaki - Fried Cheese

Serves: 6
Preparation Time: 5 minutes
Cooking Time: 10 minutes

Ingredients
1 pound krinos kefalograviera, kasseri or graviera cheese, cut into 2-inch by ½-inch pieces
Flour (for dredging)
½ cup olive oil
2 lemons, cut into wedges
1 pinch dry Oregano
Grilled or toasted pita bread (optional)

Directions
1. Rinse each piece of cut cheese under cold tap water and coat with flour.
2. Heat the oil in a skillet and fry the cheese until it is brown on both sides.
3. Drain on paper towels, and serve with lemon wedges and sprinkle a pinch of oregano. Serve with grilled or toasted pita if desired.

Spanakopita - Spinach Pie

Serves: 8
Preparation Time: 15 minutes with overnight thawing
Cooking Time: 45 minutes

Ingredients
1 8-ounce sheet puff pastry, thawed in refrigerator overnight
2 tablespoons flour for dusting, or as needed
1 large egg, optional

For filling
1 tablespoon olive oil
1 small yellow onion, diced
1 clove garlic, minced
1 cup cottage cheese
¼ cup Parmesan cheese
2 large eggs
½ teaspoon salt
Freshly ground pepper

⅛ teaspoon ground nutmeg
2 cups frozen cut spinach, thawed in refrigerator overnight

Directions
For the filling
1. Preheat the oven to 375°F.
2. Sauté the onion and garlic in a skillet with olive oil over medium heat until soft (about 5 minutes).
3. Meanwhile, in a bowl, mix the cheeses, eggs, salt, pepper, and nutmeg together well.
4. Place thawed spinach in a colander or strainer and press out as much moisture as possible. Add it to cheese mixture.
5. Add the sautéed, softened garlic and onion. Mix well.

For the crust
6. Spread out the puff pastry over a dusted work surface, and roll into a 12-inch by 12-inch square.
7. Drape the rolled dough over a 9-inch pie pan.

For baking
8. Fill the pastry-lined pan evenly with the filling.
9. Fold the corners of the pastry back over top of the filling.
10. Brush a whisked egg over the top (optional).
11. Bake for 45 minutes.
12. Let set for 5 minutes before cutting.

Tiropita - Puff Pastry Stuffed with Cheese

Serves: 9
Preparation Time: 1 hour 10 minutes
Cooking Time: 20 minutes

Ingredients
1 8-ounce sheet puff pastry
Flour for dusting
1 large egg, beaten
2 cups feta cheese, crumbled
2 tablespoons poppy or sesame seeds (optional)
1 large egg, beaten, for glaze

Directions

1. Line a baking sheet with parchment paper, and set it aside.
2. Stir the beaten egg and crumbled feta together in a bowl until mixed well.
3. Lay the puff pastry on a floured surface or cutting board, and cut it into 9 squares.
4. Place a heaping tablespoon of feta filling onto one half of the square. Leave about a 1/2-inch allowance around the edges for sealing the dough.
5. Fold the dough over to make a triangle and press the edges to seal. Place it on the lined baking sheet.
6. Repeat until all the squares have been filled.
7. Refrigerate until firm to the touch (about 1 hour) or freeze for later use.
8. Preheat the oven to 425°F.
9. Brush the tops of the pies with beaten egg and sprinkle with poppy or sesame seeds, if desired.
10. Bake until golden brown (browns easily within about 15 minutes or less). If frozen, do not thaw before baking.
11. Keeps at room temperature for two days.

Feta Fries

Serves: 6-8
Preparation Time: 5 minutes
Cooking Time: 15-30 minutes

Ingredients
1 32-ounce bag french fries
Oil for frying
½ tablespoon oregano
1 teaspoon parsley
1 teaspoon thyme
⅓ cup feta, crumbled
Kosher salt, to taste
Freshly ground pepper

Directions

1. Combine the oregano, parsley, thyme, and feta in a bowl. Season with salt (not too much) and pepper, as desired.
2. Fry the french fries according to the packaging instructions. Drain over paper towels. (You may also brush them with olive oil and bake them at 400°F for about 30 minutes, flipping once after about 20 minutes).
3. Sprinkle with the feta mixture and serve.

Zucchini Fritters

Serves: 6-12
Preparation Time: 5 minutes plus 10 minutes standing time
Cooking Time: 15-30 minutes

Ingredients
2 medium zucchini, trimmed and shredded
1 teaspoon salt
2 scallions, minced
2 tablespoons fresh dill, minced
½ cup feta cheese, crumbled
1 clove garlic, minced or pressed through a garlic press
¼ teaspoon black pepper
¼ cup cornstarch
½ teaspoon baking powder
6 tablespoons olive oil, divided
2 large eggs, beaten
Lemon wedges, for serving

Directions

1. Add salt to the shredded zucchini and toss it in a strainer over a bowl. Let it sit for 10 minutes, then press down or squeeze with your hands to remove the excess liquid.
2. In a large bowl, combine the zucchini, scallions, dill, feta, garlic, and black pepper.
3. Sprinkle the cornstarch and baking powder over the mixture and stir well.
4. In a non-stick skillet, heat 3 tablespoons of olive oil over medium heat.
5. Spoon 2 tablespoons of the zucchini mixture into the skillet, spreading into a circle and pressing down to make 2-inch-wide fritters.
6. Fry for about 2-3 minutes on both sides. Drain on paper towels.
7. Add the remaining oil and continue frying the rest of the zucchini mixture into fritters.
8. Serve with lemon wedges.

Fried Calamari

Serves: 4-8
Preparation Time: 10 minutes
Cooking Time: 15 minutes

Ingredients
25 ounces calamari, cleaned, washed and drained
1 tablespoon freshly ground pepper
2 tablespoons salt
½ tablespoon paprika
1 tablespoon oregano
¾ cup bread flour
½ cup semolina flour
Oil for frying
Lemon wedges

Directions

1. Cut the calamari into 1/2-inch rings and drain them on paper towels, but do not pat them dry.
2. Crush the seasonings into a powder using a mortar and pestle, food processor, or blender.
3. Combine the seasonings with the flours in a resealable bag or plastic container.
4. Add the calamari rings to the flour mixture and shake to coat.
5. Remove the rings from the flour mixture and gently shake off any excess flour. Arrange them on a plate.
6. Heat 2 or 3 inches of oil in a deep pan or fryer.
7. When the oil begins to bubble, test with one ring. The calamari should sizzle. This means the oil is the right temperature.
8. Fry the calamari in batches (not too many at the time, to get more crispy results), for about 2-3 minutes or until golden brown.
9. Remove from the oil using a strainer or slotted spoon and drain on paper towels.
10. Serve with squeezed lemon.

Salads

Eggplant Salad (Melitzanosalata)

Serves: 1-2
Preparation Time: 20 minutes
Cooking Time: 1 hour

Ingredients
3 eggplants, washed and pierced all over with a fork
2 cloves garlic, crushed
Parsley sprigs, finely chopped
Salt
Ground black pepper
3 tablespoons olive oil
2 tablespoons red wine vinegar, or according to taste
½ cup feta cheese

Directions

1. Preheat the oven to 350°F.
2. Bake the pierced eggplants for about 1 hour. The eggplant should be soft, with the skin slightly burnt.
3. Skin the eggplants and chop them finely.
4. Mix the eggplants, garlic, parsley, salt, and pepper well in a bowl.
5. Gradually stir in the olive oil then add the vinegar.
6. The eggplants should be almost mushy, but still slightly chunky as well.
7. Stir in the crumbled feta.

Tomato Greek Salad

Serves: 6
Preparation Time: 2 hours marinating time (or less)
Cooking Time: 0 minutes

Ingredients
4 fresh tomatoes, chopped
1 cucumber, peeled and chopped
1 green bell pepper, cut into ½-inch pieces
½ cup red onion, chopped
¼ cup Kalamata olives
½ cup feta cheese, crumbled

For the dressing
1 tablespoon red wine vinegar
1 tablespoon balsamic vinegar
1 tablespoon extra-virgin olive oil
1 teaspoon salt
1 tablespoon fresh oregano, chopped

Directions

1. Whisk the ingredients for the dressing together.
2. Toss in the rest of the ingredients.
3. Marinate for 2 hours (or less) in refrigerator for flavors to meld.
4. Serve.

Santorini Salad

Serves: 2
Preparation Time: 5 minutes
Cooking Time: 0 minutes

Ingredients
½ cucumber, peeled, halved and sliced
½ red onion, thinly sliced
¾ green bell pepper, thinly sliced
½ cup Greek olives
½ cup cherry tomatoes, halved
2 teaspoons olive oil
1 teaspoon oregano
1 tablespoon dill, chopped
Salt and pepper
1 slice of feta cheese
1 tablespoon capers

Directions

1. Toss all the ingredients together in a bowl EXCEPT the feta and capers.
2. Lay the feta cheese on top, sprinkle with capers and serve.

Classic Greek Salad

Serves: 6
Preparation Time: 20 minutes plus 30 minutes sitting time
Cooking Time: 0 minutes

Ingredients
1 cucumber, unpeeled, seeded, and sliced ¼-inch thick
1 red bell pepper, diced
1 yellow bell pepper, deced
1 cup cherry tomatoes, halved
½ red onion, sliced in half-rounds
8 ounces feta cheese, ½-inch diced
½ cup Kalamata olives, pitted

For vinaigrette
2 cloves garlic, minced
1 teaspoon dried oregano
½ teaspoon Dijon mustard
¼ cup red wine vinegar

1 teaspoon kosher salt
½ teaspoon freshly ground black pepper
½ cup olive oil

Directions

1. Whisk together all the vinaigrette ingredients, EXCEPT the olive oil, in a small bowl.
2. Gradually add the olive oil, whisking continuously, to make an emulsion. Set it aside.
3. Combine the cucumber, peppers, tomatoes, and red onion in a large bowl.
4. Pour the vinaigrette over the vegetables, and toss in the feta and olives.
5. Let it sit, unrefrigerated, for 30 minutes to allow flavors to meld.

Kolonaki Salad – Greek Salad with Roasted Chicken

Serves: 6
Preparation Time: 20 minutes plus 30 minutes to 4 hours marinating time
Cooking Time: 10 minutes

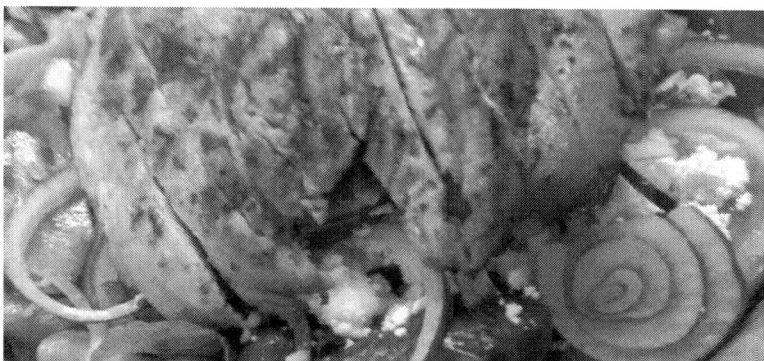

Ingredients
1 recipe Greek Salad
4 chicken breast fillets

For marinade
1 lemon, juiced
2 tablespoons extra-virgin olive oil
1 teaspoon dried oregano
Salt, to taste

10 grinds black pepper

Directions
1. Prepare the chicken marinade by mixing all the marinade ingredients together in a plastic, glass, stainless steel or other non-reactive dish.
2. Place the chicken fillets in the marinade and rub it into the chicken.
3. Cover with plastic wrap and refrigerate.
4. Marinate for 30 minutes to 4 hours.
5. Prepare the Greek salad and set it aside.
6. When chicken is ready, heat a non-stick or heavy-bottomed skillet over high heat.
7. Cook the chicken for about 4-5 minutes and turn over to cook the other side, also for 4-5 minutes. Make sure it is cooked through.
8. Place the chicken on a cutting board and let it rest for about 5 minutes.
9. Slice it into thin strips and arrange it over the Greek salad.
10. Serve.

Marouli Salad

Serves: 6
Preparation Time: 10 minutes
Cooking Time: 0 minutes

Ingredients
1 head romaine lettuce
4 scallions, chopped
3 tablespoons fresh dill, chopped
Olive oil
White wine vinegar
Salt
Juice of 1 lemon (optional)

Directions
1. Clean the lettuce by washing the leaves thoroughly with cold water. Drain well.
2. Chop the lettuce finely.
3. Toss the lettuce, scallions, and dill in a bowl.
4. Add the lemon juice (optional), together with salt, olive oil, and vinegar to taste.

Soups

Avgolemono - Lemon-Chicken-Rice Soup

Serves: 4-6
Preparation Time: 15 minutes
Cooking Time: 20 minutes

Ingredients

6 cups chicken broth
1 teaspoon fresh dill, finely chopped
½ cup uncooked orzo or rice-shaped pasta
4 large eggs
⅓ cup fresh lemon juice
1 large carrot, peeled and shredded
¼ teaspoon salt
¼ teaspoon white pepper
8 ounces chicken breast fillet, cut into bite-sized pieces

Directions

1. In a large saucepan, combine the chicken broth and dill.
2. Bring it to a boil. Add the orzo and reduce the heat.
3. Simmer for 5 minutes or until the orzo is slightly tender. Remove from the heat.
4. Place the eggs and lemon juice in a blender and process until smooth.
5. While the blender is on, slowly add most of the broth (making sure there is no orzo). Blend until smooth, and set it aside.
6. Meanwhile, add carrot, salt, pepper, and chicken to remaining broth-orzo mixture.
7. Bring it to a simmer over medium-low heat.
8. Simmer until the chicken and orzo are done (about 5 minutes).
9. Reduce the heat to low, and slowly stir in egg the mixture from the blender.
10. Cook 30 seconds more, stirring constantly.
11. Serve immediately.

Domatosoupa - Tomato Soup

Serves: 4
Preparation Time: 20 minutes
Cooking Time: 1 hour

Ingredients

3 sundried tomatoes, snipped
½ cup boiling water
1 large sweet onion, peeled and finely chopped
1 medium leek, washed and finely chopped, whites only
3 tablespoons olive oil
1 4 ½-ounce can diced tomatoes, with the juice
1 teaspoon sugar
1 garlic clove, minced
Zest of ½ an orange, grated
2 tablespoons fresh mint, finely chopped
4 ½ cups herb broth (store bought or homemade) or vegetable broth

1 ½ cups Greek yogurt
1 tablespoon all-purpose flour
Salt and freshly ground black pepper, to taste
½ cup flat leaf parsley, minced

Directions
1. Soak the sundried tomatoes in the boiling water to soften. Drain the water.
2. Pound the sundried tomatoes, with their liquid, in a mortar and pestle, until a paste is formed.
3. In a heavy-bottomed pot, sauté the onion and leek in the olive oil until translucent.
4. Add the diced tomatoes, sundried tomato paste, and sugar.
5. Cook over moderately high heat for 2-3 minutes.
6. Stir in the garlic, grated orange zest, and mint, and cook another 3 minutes.
7. Gradually add the herb or vegetable broth, cover, and simmer for 30-45 minutes longer.
8. Mix the yogurt and flour in a bowl until smooth.
9. Gradually add a spoonful of hot soup, stirring constantly.
10. Add another spoonful of soup, still stirring.
11. Slowly add the yogurt mixture to the soup pot, stirring constantly.
12. Continue cooking the soup over low heat, stirring constantly. There should be no curdling.
13. Adjust the seasonings according to taste.
14. Garnish with parsley and serve while hot.

Sandwiches/Wraps

Chicken Gyro Pita Sandwich

Serves: 2
Preparation Time: 5 minutes
Cooking Time: 0 minutes

Ingredients

1 recipe chicken gyro
2 cooked gyro or pita bread
½ cup cucumber, chopped
⅓ cup yogurt
¼ teaspoon dill weed
1 clove garlic, minced
½ small red onion, thinly sliced
1 small tomato, chopped (optional)
⅓ cup shredded lettuce (optional)

Directions

1. In a bowl, combine the cucumber, yogurt, dill, and garlic. Set aside.
2. Spoon some of the chicken gyro onto a piece of gyro or pita bread. Add some of the cucumber mixture, onion, tomato (optional) and lettuce (optional).
3. Fold over or roll into a wrap and serve.

Greek Sausage Sandwich

Serves: 8
Preparation Time: 10 minutes
Cooking Time: 5 minutes

Ingredients
Feta sauce
1 ½ cups sour cream or Greek yogurt
1 cup feta cheese
½ teaspoon garlic powder
½ teaspoon oregano
Salt and pepper to taste

For sandwiches
8 pita bread
2 pounds bulk loukaniko sausage, halved lengthwise and sliced
1 long thin cucumber, diced
1 cup lettuce, shredded
4 small tomatoes, diced
2 small red onions, sliced thinly

Directions

1. Mix the sauce ingredients together and set them aside for the flavors to develop.
2. Sauté the sausage slices and in a skillet over medium heat until browned. Remove from skillet and set aside.
3. Add onions to the skillet and cook 1-2 minutes until fragrant and soft. Drain any excess fat.
4. Grill the pita in a non-stick skillet over medium-low heat or in a sandwich press to the desired crispness.
5. Layer sausage, tomato, cucumber, lettuce, and caramelized onions inside the bread.
6. Top with about a tablespoon feta sauce.

Pork Souvlaki Pita Sandwich

Serves: 6
Preparation Time: 10 minutes
Cooking Time: 12 minutes

Ingredients

1 recipe pork souvlaki
6 pita breads
2 cups shredded green leaf lettuce
1 small white onion, thinly sliced into half moons
3 large round tomatoes, medium dice
½ cup olive oil
3 tablespoons red wine vinegar
1 teaspoon dried oregano
Salt and freshly ground black pepper, to taste
Tzatziki or feta sauce or crumbled feta cheese (optional)

Directions

1. Preheat the grill to medium-high, and cook the pork until done (remove any skewers after grilling) or fry it in a lightly oiled skillet over medium-high heat.
2. In a medium bowl, toss the lettuce, onion, tomatoes, olive oil, vinegar, oregano, salt, and pepper together.
3. Spoon the meat into a piece of pita (grilled, if desired) and top with lettuce mixture and tzatziki, feta sauce, or crumbled feta cheese (optional). Serve.

Santorini Wrap – Grilled Vegetable and Feta Sandwich

Serves: 3
Preparation Time: 5 minutes
Cooking Time: 8 minutes

Ingredients

3 whole pitas, warmed or toasted

For filling
3 tablespoons olive oil
1 small eggplant, cut into ½-inch by 3-inch strips
1 small red bell pepper, cut into ½-inch by 3-inch strips
1 small zucchini, cut into ½-inch by 3-inch strips
1 small onion, cut into ½-inch by 3-inch strips
1 clove garlic, minced

¼ cup green olives, halved
¼ cup Kalamata olives, halved
¼ cup feta cheese, crumbled
3 tablespoons pepperoncini, sliced

Directions

1. Heat a large skillet over medium heat and add the olive oil.
2. Sauté the eggplant and zucchini strips until tender (about 4 minutes).
3. Add the pepper slices, onion, and garlic.
4. Cover and let it cook until the vegetables have softened (about 4 minutes).
5. Remove from the heat and stir in the olives, pepperoncini, and feta.
6. Slice the pita to make pockets and stuff with the filling.

Greek Burger with Kefalotyri

Serves: 12
Preparation Time: 15 minutes
Cooking Time: 12 minute (on grill or skillet) or 1 hour (in oven)

Ingredients
12 pieces bread of choice (burger buns or pita)
4 small tomatoes, sliced

For patties
1 cup *kefalotyri* cheese, grated
1 pound ground beef
1 medium onion, finely chopped
½ carrot, grated
2 sprigs parsley, finely chopped
½ teaspoon spearmint
½ teaspoon oregano
½ teaspoon paprika
½ salt or to taste
½ teaspoon pepper

1 egg, beaten

1 loaf or 10-12 slices crustless bread, slightly soaked and strained well

1 tablespoon olive oil

Juice of ½ an orange

Dried bread crumbs, as needed

Directions

1. Combine all the patties' ingredients until thoroughly blended EXCEPT the *kefalotyri* cheese and dry bread crumbs. Gradually add some dry breadcrumbs if too moist or sticky.
2. If baking, preheat the oven to 375°F.
3. Divide the meat mixture into 12 portions and form each into a patty.
4. Sprinkle each patty with kefalotyri.
5. Place patties on a baking sheet and bake for about 1 hour or until cooked through.
6. May also be cooked on a grill or in a skillet over medium-high heat (about 3 minutes). Flip over until some bits of meat are slightly charred and of desired doneness. Sprinkle with cheese just before removing from heat.
7. Place in the bread and serve topped with tomato and tzatziki, if desired.

Basic Greek Pita Bread

Serves: 8-16
Preparation Time: 25 minutes plus 1 hour proofing time
Cooking Time: 20 minutes

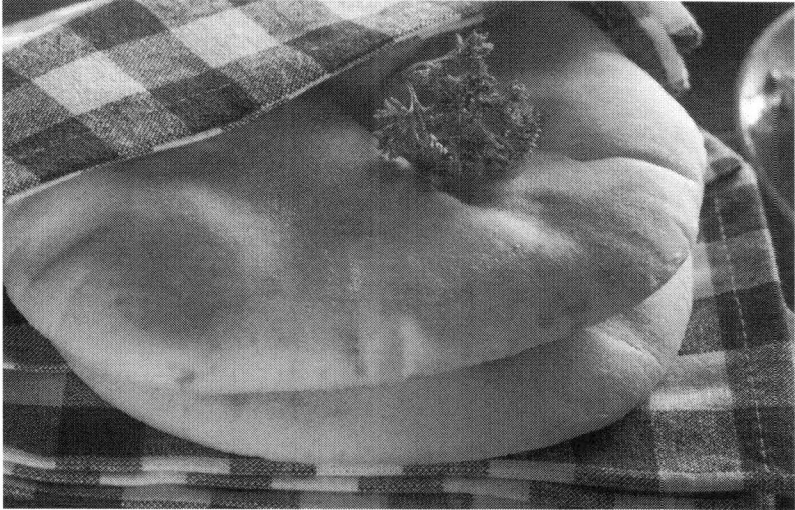

Ingredients

4 cups all-purpose flour + more, if needed
2 teaspoons fresh thyme, chopped (optional)
1 tablespoon olive oil + more for brushing

For yeast
1 envelope (7 g or 2 ¼ teaspoons) dry yeast
1 tablespoon sugar
½ cup warm (not hot) water

For salt
1 cup warm water
2 teaspoons salt

Directions

1. In a small bowl, stir together the yeast, sugar, and warm water. Let stand for 10 minutes. Froth on the surface indicates that the yeast is activated.
2. In another small bowl or cup, dissolve the salt in the water.
3. In a third large bowl, add the flour and thyme, if using. Make a large well in the center and pour in the yeast mixture.
4. Mix in about 3 strokes with a wooden spoon or with the hook attachment of your mixer before adding the salt and water solution.
5. Mix for a minute or two until everything is combined. Add more flour, gradually, if the dough is too sticky, or gradually add water if it is too dry.
6. Knead into a smooth dough (about 15 minutes). The dough should retract when pinched.
7. Gradually knead the oil into the dough until well incorporated.
8. Brush a clean, dry bowl with oil and place the dough inside.
9. Brush the surface of the dough with a little more oil and cover the bowl with a towel or aluminum foil.
10. Let it sit in a warm place. Allow the dough to expand to double its size (about 40 minutes to 2 hours, depending on ambient or room temperature).
11. Punch the dough down, and knead quickly or press down (about 2 minutes) to deflate the dough.
12. Form the dough into a flat rectangle and divide it into 8-16 pieces (or more), depending on the desired size. Shape the pieces into balls.
13. Cover the balls and let them rest for 30 minutes.

14. Flatten the balls and use a rolling pin to shape them into circles about ¼-inch thick. Rest the rounds for about 5 minutes before cooking. You may also place them in a sealed container and refrigerate for later use.
15. While cooking, cover uncooked rounds of dough with towels to prevent them from drying out.
16. To cook the pitas, brush them with oil, and fry them in a pan over medium heat. When they puff up, flip them over (about 2 minutes on each side). Alternatively, you can bake them on oiled baking sheets at 350°F, for about 2-3 minutes.
17. May be eaten as is or with tzatziki, used to make wraps, or slit to make a pocket and filled with meat and/or vegetables.

Beef/Lamb/Pork

Pork Souvlaki

Serves: 6

Preparation Time: 20 minutes plus 3 hours marinating time

Cooking Time: 12 minutes

Ingredients

2 pounds pork shoulder, cut into 1 ¼-inch cubes
For marinade
½ cup lemon juice
2 tablespoons red wine vinegar
2 tablespoons fresh oregano, chopped
1 tablespoon fresh thyme, chopped
1 bay leaf, finely crumbled
6 cloves garlic, minced
3 tablespoons olive oil
Salt, to taste
Freshly ground black pepper, to taste
Lemon wedges, for serving (optional)

Directions

1. Prepare at least 6 skewers. If they are made of wood, soak for 1 hour in water before use.
2. Combine the ingredients for the marinade (do not include lemon wedges) in a bowl or resealable bag. Add the pork cubes and seal, and marinate for at least 3 hours to overnight.
3. Skewer the meat and grill over medium-high heat, brushing occasionally with marinade until done (about 10 minutes). Be sure to allow the last application of marinade to cook before removing from the heat.
4. May be served with lemon wedges to be squeezed on the meat before eating.

Beef Kebab

Serves: 4
Preparation Time: 5 minutes
Cooking Time: 12 minutes

Ingredients
2 pounds beef sirloin, cut into about 1 ½-inch cubes
2 bell peppers, seeded and cut into 1 ½-inch squares
1 large onion cut into 1 ½-inch squares
Lemon wedges

For marinade
2 tablespoons olive oil
2 tablespoons red wine vinegar
2 tablespoons lemon juice
3 cloves garlic, minced
1 tablespoon oregano
1 tablespoon dried mint
2 teaspoons kosher salt
½ teaspoon chili flakes

Directions

1. Whisk the ingredients for the marinade together. Place it in a resealable bag or shallow pan.
2. Add the meat and seal. Marinate for 30 minutes to overnight, flipping once or twice.
3. If using wooden skewers, soak them in water for 1 hour before using.
4. After marinating, preheat the grill to high.
5. Thread the meat alternately with the bell pepper onto the skewers, being careful not to crowd them too much.
6. Grill for 8-12 minutes, brushing with marinade and rotating once halfway through the cooking process.
7. Let rest for 5 minutes before serving.
8. Serve with lemon wedges to squeeze over kebabs.

Lamb Chops

Serves: 4

Preparation Time: 5 minutes plus at least 30 minutes marinating time

Cooking Time: 6 minutes

Ingredients

¼ cup dried oregano

2 tablespoons lemon juice

1 tablespoon garlic, minced

Salt and freshly ground pepper

8 lamb loin chops, trimmed

Directions

1. Mix the oregano, lemon juice, garlic, salt, and pepper together. Rub the spice mix on the lamb chops.
2. Cover, refrigerate, and let marinate for 30 minutes to 4 hours.

3. Grill or broil the lamb chops over medium-high heat for 3 minutes on each side or longer, depending on desired doneness.

Beefteki - Feta Burger

Serves: 4
Preparation Time: 5 minutes
Cooking Time: 16 minutes

Ingredients

1 pound lean ground beef
½ teaspoon Worcestershire sauce
1 teaspoon dried parsley
Salt and pepper to taste
1 cup crumbled feta cheese

Directions

1. Preheat the grill to medium, and oil the grate.
2. Set aside the feta cheese, and mix all the other ingredients thoroughly.
3. Divide the mixture into 8 balls and form into thin patties.
4. Put about ¼ cup of the feta cheese on 4 of the patties.
5. Top each with another patty, pressing down on the sides to seal.
6. Cook on the preheated grill for about 8 minutes per side, or until well done (160°F internal temperature).
7. Serve with baked lemon potatoes.

Classic Moussaka

Serves: 4
Preparation Time: 1 hour
Cooking Time: 45 minutes

Ingredients
2 medium potatoes, peeled and cut into ¼-inch circles
2-3 medium eggplants, peeled and cut into about ⅛-inch circles
Olive oil, as needed

For beef-tomato mixture
1 pound lean ground beef or lamb
1 ½ medium onions, peeled and chopped
2 tablespoons garlic, minced
1 8-ounce can tomato sauce
1 teaspoon dried oregano
2 tablespoons dried parsley
¼ teaspoon cinnamon
¼ teaspoon nutmeg

¼ teaspoon sugar

½ teaspoon salt, or to taste

½ teaspoon fresh ground black pepper, or to taste

For white sauce

3 tablespoons butter

½ teaspoon salt

½ teaspoon fresh ground black pepper

2 tablespoons flour

1 cup half-and-half cream or milk

2 eggs, beaten

½ cup grated Parmesan cheese

Directions

For potato and eggplant layers

1. Preheat the oven to 450°F, and grease a 9x13 or lasagna pan.
2. Arrange the potato slices on the bottom of the pan as the first layer. Brush with olive oil.
3. Place the eggplant slices on top of the potato as a second layer. Again, brush with olive oil.
4. Bake for 15 minutes.
5. When eggplant and potato are tender, remove them from the oven. Separate a few slices of eggplant to make another layer for later.
6. Reduce the heat to 350°F.

For beef-tomato sauce layer

7. Brush a large skillet with oil and heat over medium-high on the stovetop.
8. Cook the beef and onions, stirring until the beef is no longer pink and the onions are soft. Skim off any excess fat or grease from skillet.

9. Add the garlic, tomato sauce, oregano, parsley, cinnamon, nutmeg, sugar, salt and black pepper. Stir until heated through.
10. Pour the beef-tomato sauce mixture over the layer of potatoes and eggplant in the pan.
11. Arrange the remaining eggplant slices over the beef mixture.

For the white sauce
12. In a saucepan, melt the butter over medium-low heat and whisk in the flour, salt and pepper to taste.
13. Gradually whisk in half-and-half or milk.
14. Adjust the heat to medium high and cook, with continuous stirring, until the sauce is thick and bubbly. Reduce the heat (or turn it off) to avoid scorching while preparing the cheese mixture.
15. Put the beaten eggs in a small bowl and stir in the hot milky sauce about a tablespoon at a time (do not add too much hot sauce all at once or the eggs will cook and harden). Add about 4 tablespoons of the hot milky sauce, stirring continuously. Stir in the Parmesan cheese as well.
16. Stir this cheese sauce into the milky sauce. Cook a little longer, if needed, until the mixture begins to thicken. Pour this over the contents of the baking dish.
17. Bake in the preheated oven for 45 minutes.
18. Remove from the oven and let it sit for about 15-30 minutes, to set, before slicing.

Greek-Style Stuffed Peppers

Serves: 8
Preparation Time: 20 minutes
Cooking Time: 20 minutes sautéing plus 40 minutes baking

Ingredients

8 medium-sized bell peppers, any color, tops removed, seeded
1 tablespoon olive oil
½ pound ground pork
2 onions, chopped
Salt and pepper to taste
¼ cup dry white wine
1 10.75-ounce can tomato puree
1 4-ounce package feta cheese
½ cup cooked white rice
½ cup raisins
½ cup pine nuts
2 tablespoons fresh parsley, chopped

Directions

1. Preheat the oven to 350°F.
2. Soak the bell peppers in warm water for 5 minutes.
3. Heat the olive oil in a skillet over medium heat.
4. Sauté the pork and onions, seasoning with salt and pepper, until the pork is evenly browned.
5. Transfer the sautéed pork and onion to a clean skillet or simply drain out the grease.
6. Stir in the wine and tomato puree and simmer for 10 minutes. Remove from the heat.
7. Add the feta cheese, cooked rice, raisins, pine nuts, and parsley, mixing thoroughly.
8. Stuff the peppers with pork mixture,
9. Arrange the stuffed peppers in a baking dish, and cover lid or with aluminum foil.
10. Bake for 30 minutes.
11. Remove the lid or foil, and continue baking until the stuffing is lightly browned (about 10 minutes).

Loukaniko - Homemade Greek Pork Sausage

Serves: 15-20
Preparation Time: 15 minutes plus 3 hours sitting time
Cooking Time: 10-15 minutes

Ingredients
5 pounds ground pork shoulder, chilled (you may use lamb or a combination)
Hog casing (optional)

For seasoning
2 tablespoons garlic, finely minced
1 tablespoon dried thyme
1 tablespoon dried marjoram
1 tablespoons grated orange zest
1 tablespoon ground coriander seed
1 tablespoon dried oregano

1 tablespoon black pepper

1 tablespoon salt

1 tablespoon sugar (optional)

½ cup dry white or red wine

Directions

1. Keep the ground meat in the refrigerator until ready to use (cold meat is important for better binding).
2. Mix together all the ingredients for the seasoning and let it stand for 1 hour to allow flavors to meld.
3. Add the seasoning to the chilled ground pork, and mix thoroughly with your hands.
4. Stuff hog casings with sausage meat, or use a pastry tube, to make 6-inch long sausages. You can also make patties, or roll in saran wrap for skinless sausages.
5. Keep the sausages in the freezer overnight before cooking.
6. You can bake, grill or fry the sausage. It should be cooked until the surface looks almost charred.

Lamb Shanks

Serves: 6
Preparation Time:
Cooking Time: 2 ½-3 hours

Ingredients
6 lamb shanks (14-ounce pieces)
Salt, to taste
Freshly ground black pepper, to taste
Flour, for dusting
3 tablespoons olive oil
2 celery stalks, chopped
1 large onion, chopped
1 large carrot, chopped
6 large cloves garlic, chopped

1 2-ounce can anchovies

2 cinnamon sticks

2 small bay leaves

Handful of fresh thyme sprigs

2 tablespoons gin

¼ teaspoon ground nutmeg

1 tablespoon tomato paste

1 25-ounce bottle Merlot

2 14-ounce cans low-salt beef broth

1 cup Kalamata olives (optional)

Directions

1. Preheat the oven to 325°F, and grease a baking pan.
2. Pat the lamb shanks dry with towels. Rub with salt and pepper and then dust with flour.
3. Heat the oil in large ovenproof pot over medium-high heat.
4. Sauté the lamb until browned evenly (about 10 minutes). Transfer it to the greased baking pan and place it in oven to bake, as you prepare the sauce.
5. Add the next 10 ingredients (celery through nutmeg) to the pot.
6. Sauté until the vegetables start to brown (about 20 minutes).
7. Stir in the tomato paste, wine, and broth.
8. Simmer until the liquid is reduced by half, stirring occasionally (about 10 minutes).
9. Return the lamb to the pot of sauce, and arrange it in a single layer.
10. Bring it to a boil.

11. Transfer the whole pot, with the lamb, to the oven. Cook, uncovered, until tender (about 2-3 hours). Flip the shanks over and baste them from time to time.
12. Remove the lamb and place it on a plate.
13. Skim any fat from the liquid and strain out the vegetable pieces, catching the liquid in a bowl.
14. Pour the strained liquid back into the pot and boil to reduce it further, if needed, to gravy consistency. Season with salt and pepper.
15. Return the lamb to the pot of gravy and cook until heated through.
16. Serve with baked lemon potatoes.

Chicken/Poultry

Greek-Style Grilled Chicken

Serves: 4
Preparation Time: 10 minutes plus overnight marinating time
Cooking Time: 45 minutes

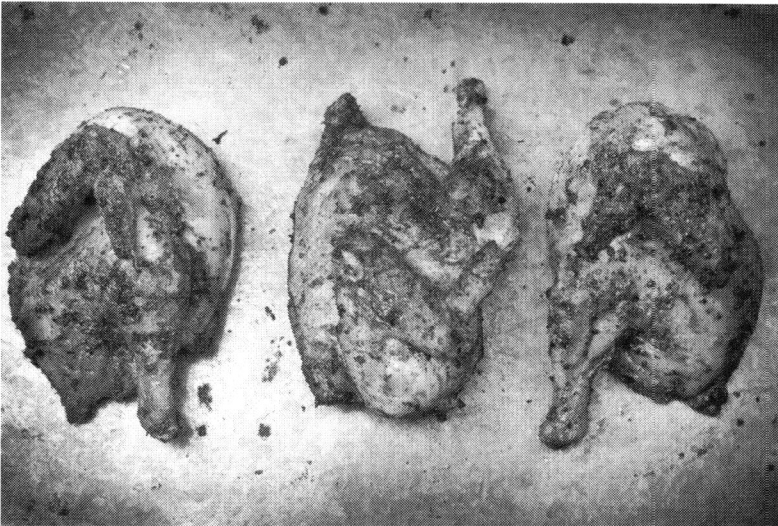

Ingredients
½ cup extra-virgin olive oil
1 bunch fresh oregano, leaves picked
4 cloves garlic, finely minced
Juice of 1 lemon
Salt and freshly ground black pepper, to taste
1 whole chicken, cut in pieces

Directions

1. Pat the chicken dry and place it in a resealable bag or shallow container for marinating.
2. Whisk together the rest of the ingredients and pour them over the chicken.
3. Seal and turn the bag over several times to distribute the marinade over the chicken pieces.
4. Refrigerate and let marinate overnight.
5. After marinating, preheat the oven to 350°F.
6. Heat a skillet over medium-high heat and place the chicken skin-side down.
7. Brown the chicken (about 10 minutes on each side).
8. Place the chicken on a baking tray and bake in oven until golden brown (about 25 minutes).
9. Remove from the oven and let rest for 10 minutes.
10. Serve.

Chicken Gyro

Serves: 2
Preparation Time: 5 minutes plus 1 hour marinating time
Cooking Time: 8 minutes

Ingredients
½ pound chicken boneless breast, cut into ½-inch strips

For marinade
¼ cup lemon juice
2 tablespoons olive oil
1 clove garlic, minced
½ teaspoon ground mustard
½ teaspoon dried oregano

Directions

1. Combine the ingredients for the marinade in a resealable bag.
2. Add the chicken, refrigerate, and let marinade for at least 1 hour, flipping the bag over once or twice to make sure the chicken absorbs the flavor evenly.
3. After the marinating is done, drain and discard the marinade.
4. Heat a nonstick skillet over medium heat and cook the chicken for about 8 minutes, stirring occasionally, or until done.

Baked Chicken with Rosemary and Lemon

Serves: 4-6
Preparation Time: 15 minutes
Cooking Time: 1 hour

Ingredients
1 whole chicken (5 pounds), washed and drained
Salt and pepper
Juice of 2 lemons

For basting
2 tablespoons olive oil
½ cup butter, softened
2 large sprigs fresh rosemary, diced finely
4 cloves garlic, minced
Zest of 4 lemons

For stuffing
1 lemon, sliced
1 small onion, quartered
1 sprig rosemary

Directions
1. Preheat the oven to 425°F.
2. In a bowl, mix the basting ingredients together.
3. Wipe the chicken dry and rub it with salt and pepper; season the cavity as well.
4. Stuff the cavity of the chicken with the sliced lemon, onion, and rosemary.
5. Brush the chicken with the basting mixture.
6. Place the chicken on a baking sheet or tray, and bake for 45 minutes.
7. Remove from the oven and baste again with remaining basting mixture.
8. Put back into oven and bake until golden brown (about 15 minutes). Cover with foil to prevent burning, if needed.
9. Cool for 15 minutes before serving.

Seafood

Shrimp Kebabs

Serves: 2
Preparation Time: 10 minutes
Cooking Time: 6 minutes

Ingredients
1 pound shrimp, shelled and deveined
Olive oil, as needed
½ teaspoon aniseed, finely crushed
Salt
Freshly-ground pepper
4 tablespoons tzatziki
¾ cup feta, crumbled

Directions

1. Preheat the grill to medium-high heat, and brush the rack with oil.
2. Thread the shrimp onto 4 metal or soaked wooden skewers.
3. Brush the shrimp with olive oil, and season with salt, pepper, and aniseed.
4. Grill until shrimp are opaque in center (about 3 minutes per side).
5. Spoon the tzatziki over the shrimp and sprinkle it with feta cheese.
6. Serve with Greek salad.

Grilled Salmon

Serves: 4
Preparation Time: 20 minutes
Cooking Time: 20 minutes

Ingredients
4 salmon fillets (about 1 pound)

For marinade
1 tablespoon olive oil
1 tablespoon fresh dill, chopped
1 teaspoon grated lemon peel
3 tablespoons lemon juice
2 tablespoons honey
2 cloves garlic, minced

Lemon-Dill Sauce

1 6-ounce container Greek yogurt, plain
1 tablespoon fresh dill, chopped
½ teaspoon grated lemon peel
1 tablespoon lemon juice
⅛ teaspoon pepper

Directions

1. Whisk the marinade ingredients together. Set aside.
2. In a baking dish, arrange the salmon skin-side up.
3. Pour the marinade over the salmon. Turn the fillets over, and then cover with plastic wrap.
4. Let the fish marinate in the refrigerator for 20 minutes.
5. Preheat the grill to medium heat.
6. Brush the grill rack with oil and place the salmon skin-side down on grill.
7. Cover and grill until the fish flakes easily (about 10-15 minutes).
8. While grilling the salmon, whisk together the lemon-dill sauce ingredients.
9. Serve grilled salmon with sauce.

Grilled Greek-Style Fish

Serves: 2
Preparation Time: 5 minutes
Cooking Time: 25 minutes

Ingredients

1-2 whole porgy fishes, trimmed and cleaned, about 1 ½ pound each
Salt and pepper to taste
Greek extra-virgin olive oil
Dry oregano

Lemon oil
1 cup Greek olive oil
1 lemon juiced
Lemon wedges for serving

Directions

1. Prepare the barbecue or indoor grill to high heat
2. Score the fish on both side.
3. Brush some olive oil on both side of the fish. Season with salt on both side and inside the fish. Sprinkle a pinch of dry oregano on both side of each fish.
4. Place each fish in a fish grilling basket to prevent sticking to the grate. Grill for 10-20 minutes per side or until the fish is cooked through and internal temperature reaches 145°F.
5. In the meantime, prepare the lemon oil. Place olive oil in a small food processor or blender with the lemon juice. Blend until well emulsified. Add olive oil if needed. Pour in a bottle for further uses.
6. Once the fish is cooked, place it on a serving plate. Sprinkle the grilled porgies with some of the prepared lemon oil. Sprinkle with oregano and serve with lemon wedges.

Grilled Octopus

Serves: 6
Preparation Time: 15 minutes
Cooking Time: 6 minutes

Ingredients

8 ounces baby octopus, cleaned
¼ cup dry white wine
2 teaspoons extra virgin olive oil
2 cloves garlic, crushed
1 teaspoon ground mild paprika
1 small fresh red chili, finely chopped
¼ cup Greek olives
Freshly ground black pepper
Salt, to taste
Lemon wedges, to serve

Directions

1. Rinse the octopus with cold water and drain. Pat it dry with towels.
2. In a non-reactive container, mix all the ingredients, EXCEPT the lemon wedges, together.
3. Toss in the octopus and coat well with the seasonings.
4. Cover with plastic wrap and let it marinate in the refrigerator for 30 minutes.
5. Preheat the grill to high.
6. After marinating, drain the octopus but set the marinade aside to be made into sauce.
7. Cook the octopus on the grill, flipping a few times (about 5 minutes). The octopus is done when it is heated through and begins to curl.
8. Transfer the cooked octopus to a serving dish.
9. Heat up the reserved marinade over medium-high heat, and bring it to a boil. Add the Greek olives.
10. Adjust the flavor with salt and pepper, and cook for about 1 minute or until slightly thickened.
11. Pour the sauce over the octopus and serve with lemon wedges.

Stuffed Squid

Serves: 4
Preparation Time: 30 minutes
Cooking Time: 1 hour

Ingredients
8 cleaned squid, 5-6 inches each in length, cleaned and gutted, tentacles chopped

For stuffing
2 teaspoons olive oil
1 medium onion, finely chopped
1 cup cooked rice, slightly salted
¼ cup toasted pine nuts
2 tablespoons currants, soaked in water for 10 minutes and drained
¼ cup flat-leaf parsley, finely chopped
Salt, to taste
Freshly ground black pepper to taste

For sauce
1 teaspoon olive oil
¼ cup onion, finely chopped
2 cloves garlic, minced
1 14-ounce can tomatoes, drained and diced, juice reserved
½ cup dry white wine
1 ½ teaspoons fresh lemon juice
Salt, to taste
Freshly ground black pepper, to taste

Directions

1. Rinse the cleaned, gutted squid and drain. Pat it dry with towels.
2. Place the tentacles in a bowl and set them aside.
3. Heat the olive oil in a skillet and sauté the onion (about 1 minute).
4. Add the tentacles and sauté 1 minute more. Remove from the heat.
5. Add the other stuffing ingredients and mix thoroughly.
6. Stuff the squid with about 2 ½ tablespoons of the filling. Do not overstuff to avoid bursting while cooking.
7. Seal the squid using toothpicks like a pin. Set them aside and prepare the sauce.
8. Heat a large pan with a tight-fitting lid, big enough for the squid to fit in one layer.
9. Heat the oil and sauté onion and garlic until onion is soft (about 2 minutes).
10. Add remaining sauce ingredients and bring it to a simmer.
11. Add the stuffed squid to the sauce, arranging it in a single layer.

12. Bring to a simmer, then reduce the heat to low and cover the pan tightly.
13. Simmer for 50 minutes to 1 hour, depending on the size of the squids.
14. Make sure the liquid does not dry up; add water or wine to prevent drying.
15. Serve hot with some sauce.

Vegetables and Sides

Baked Lemon Potatoes

Serves: 2
Preparation Time: 5 minutes
Cooking Time: 45-50 minutes

Ingredients

1 pound potatoes, cleaned, peeled, and sliced
3 tablespoons extra-virgin olive oil
2 cloves garlic, minced
1 tablespoon Greek oregano
2 tablespoons yellow mustard
Juice of 1 lemon
¼ cup chicken or vegetable broth

Directions

1. Preheat the oven to 350°F.
2. In a bowl, combine the olive oil, garlic, oregano, mustard, and lemon juice.
3. Add the potatoes and toss well to coat. Transfer the potatoes to a baking dish.
4. Very carefully, add the broth. Do not pour over the potatoes as this will wash off the seasonings.
5. Bake the potatoes for 20-25 minutes and then stir. The potatoes should start to soften by this point.
6. Continue baking for another 20-25 minutes or until potatoes are cooked through.
7. Serve with beefteki and tzatziki.

Spanakorizo - Spinach Lemon Rice Pilaf

Serves: 3-4
Preparation Time: 5 minutes
Cooking Time: 15 minutes

Ingredients

2 tablespoons olive oil
1 small onion, diced
2 cloves garlic, minced
1 lemon, zested and juiced
3 cups cold cooked rice
½ cup vegetable or chicken stock
½ pound baby spinach
4 tablespoons fresh chopped dill, finely chopped
Salt and freshly ground black pepper, to taste
Crumble feta cheese and flat leaf parsley for garnish

Directions

1. Heat the oil in a large deep skillet over medium heat.
2. Sauté the onion and garlic until onion turns golden and soft (about 2 minutes).
3. Stir in the baby spinach and half of the dill. Continue cooking until wilted, about 2-3 minutes.
4. Break up any lumps in the cooked rice, and add it to the skillet, together with the stock and lemon juice.
5. Mix well, shovelling from bottom to top to coat the rice with oil.
6. Reduce the heat to medium-low. Add remaining dill and lemon zest. Stir to combine.
7. To serve, sprinkle the rice mixture with feta and parsley, if desired.

Note: if you don't have cooked rice on hand, increase the vegetable or chicken stock to 2 cup and add 1 cup of basmati rice to the skillet. Bring to a boil. Cover and reduce heat so the rice mixture simmer and cook for 18-20 minutes, or until the rice is cooked.

Gigantes Plaki - Butter Beans Baked in Tomato Sauce

Serves: 4
Preparation Time: 20 minutes
Cooking Time: 2 hours

Ingredients

1 ½ cups dried butter beans, soaked overnight and drained
3 tablespoons extra-virgin olive oil, or as needed
1 onion, finely chopped
2 cloves garlic, finely chopped
2 tablespoons tomato paste
4 cups ripe tomatoes, skins removed, roughly chopped
1 teaspoon sugar
1 teaspoon dried oregano
⅛ teaspoon ground cinnamon
2 tablespoons flat-leaf parsley, chopped, plus more for garnish
Salt and pepper

Directions

1. Rinse the butter beans and place them in a pot. Cover with water, and bring them to a boil.
2. Reduce the heat and simmer until the beans are tender (about 50 minutes).
3. Drain and set aside.
4. Preheat the oven to 350°F.
5. Meanwhile, heat a large skillet or frying pan over medium heat, and add the olive oil.
6. Sauté the onion and garlic until softened (about 10 minutes).
7. Stir in tomato paste and cook 1 minute.
8. Add the rest of the ingredients and simmer for 2-3 minutes.
9. Season with salt and pepper.
10. Add the beans and mix well, then transfer the mixture to a baking dish and put in the oven.
11. Bake, uncovered, until the beans are the right tenderness (about 1 hour). Do not stir while baking.
12. Remove from the oven and allow it to cool.
13. Sprinkle with parsley and drizzle with olive oil before serving.

Tzatziki - Yogurt and Cucumber Sauce

Yields about 2 cups
Preparation Time: 10 minutes
Cooking Time: 0 minutes

Ingredients
½ cucumber, peeled and seeded
¼-½ teaspoon kosher salt
Zest of 1 lemon
Juice of ½ a lemon
2 cloves garlic, crushed to a paste
1 ½ cups Greek yogurt
¼ cup fresh dill
1 teaspoon ground cumin

Directions

1. Grate the cucumber. Salt it and let it drain in a strainer for about 5 minutes.
2. Squeeze or press out as much water from the cucumber as possible (this important to get a good consistency).
3. Put all the sauce ingredients in a food processor or blender, and process until smooth.

Skordalia - Potato and Garlic Dip

Serves: 3
Preparation Time: 30 minutes
Cooking Time: 20 minutes

Ingredients

For boiling
1 pound potatoes, scrubbed
Water for boiling
Salt

For garlic-almond paste
8 garlic cloves, minced
Salt
¾ cup whole almonds, blanched
½ cup extra virgin olive oil
½ cup water

For water-vinegar mixture
1 tablespoon + 1 teaspoon salt
5 tablespoons fresh lemon juice

3 tablespoons white wine vinegar
Fresh ground black pepper

For serving
Cut vegetables
Toasted pita triangles

Directions

1. Cover the potatoes by two inches of water in a pot. Season generously with salt, and bring it to a boil.
2. Reduce the heat to a simmer and cook until the potatoes are tender (about 30 minutes).
3. Drain and let cool slightly.
4. Rub off the skins.
5. Chop the potatoes and use a food mill to puree them.
6. Place the garlic in a mortar and pestle. Sprinkle with kosher salt and pound it into a paste.
7. In a food processor, combine the garlic, almonds, oil, and water. Puree into a paste.
8. Combine the garlic-almond mixture with the potatoes. Mix well.
9. Add the water-vinegar ingredients and mix well until well incorporated.
10. Adjust the salt and pepper to taste, and serve with cut vegetables or toasted pita.

Greek-Style Mixed Grilled Vegetables

Serves: 4
Preparation Time: 10 minutes
Cooking Time: 10 minutes

Ingredients
¼ cup Greek olive oil
1 tablespoon fresh lemon juice
2 cloves garlic, minced
1 teaspoon oregano
2 small eggplants, cut into 1-inch cubes
1 bell pepper, cut into 1-inch cubes
1 zucchini, cut into 1-inch cubes
1 small onion, quartered
Salt and pepper

Directions
1. In a large bowl, whisk together the olive oil, lemon juice, garlic, and oregano.
2. Toss the cut vegetables into the oil and coat evenly.
3. Preheat the grill to medium, and place vegetables on the rack in a single layer.
4. Baste with oil and turn over once or twice. Cook until tender.
5. Serve warm.

Dessert Recipes

Baklava

Serves: 18
Preparation Time:
Cooking Time:

Ingredients
1 16-ounce package phyllo dough
1 pound chopped nuts
1 teaspoon ground cinnamon
1 cup butter, softened

For syrup or sauce

1 cup water

1 cup white sugar

1 teaspoon vanilla extract

½ cup honey

Directions

1. Preheat the oven to 350°F.
2. Butter the bottom and sides of a 9x13 pan.
3. Toss the chopped nuts with the cinnamon, and set aside.
4. Unroll the phyllo dough, and cut the whole stack in half to fit the pan.
5. Cover the phyllo with a dampened cloth or towel to keep it from drying out.
6. Place two sheets of dough in the pan, and butter thoroughly.
7. Sprinkle 2-3 tablespoons chopped nuts over the dough.
8. Repeat the layers: 2 sheets of phyllo, butter, and nuts, until you are 6-8 layers deep.
9. Using a sharp knife, cut into diamond or square shapes all the way through to the bottom of the pan.
10. Bake until the baklava is golden and crisp (about 50 minutes).
11. Prepare the syrup while the baklava is baking.
12. In a saucepan, combine the water and sugar, and bring it to a boil without mixing.
13. When the sugar has melted, add the honey and vanilla. Simmer for 20 minutes.
14. Remove the baklava from the oven and immediately spoon the syrup over it.
15. Leave it uncovered and let it cool.

Rizogalo - Rice Pudding

Serves: 6
Preparation Time: 5 minutes plus 4 hours chilling time
Cooking Time: 40 minutes

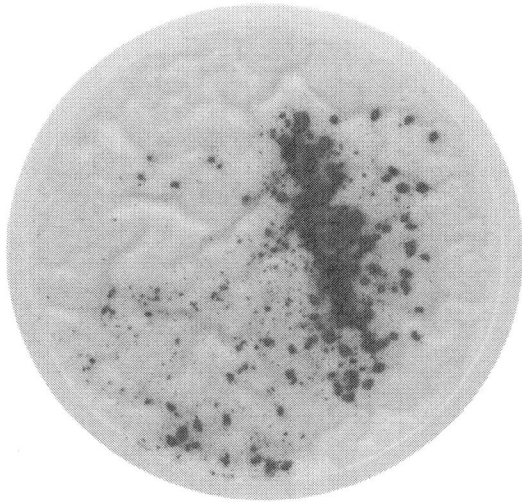

Ingredients

½ cup uncooked short-grain rice
2 cups water
2 cups milk
4 tablespoons sugar
1 teaspoon vanilla extract
Ground cinnamon

For thickener
½ cup milk
4 tablespoons cornstarch

Directions

1. In a bowl, mix the ingredients for the thickener together, and set aside.
2. Combine the rice and water in a saucepan over high heat and bring it to a boil.
3. Reduce the heat to medium low, and let it simmer, uncovered, stirring occasionally.
4. Continue simmering until the water has been absorbed and the rice is soft (about 20 minutes).
5. Add the milk and sugar, and adjust heat to high to bring it to a boil.
6. Give the thickener mixture a quick swirl and stir it into the rice.
7. Add vanilla and mix well. Remove the pot from the heat.
8. Spoon the pudding mixture into individual bowls. Sprinkle with cinnamon and cool to room temperature.
9. Chill for 4 hours and serve.

Galaktoboureko - Creamy Custard Pastry

Serves: 15
Preparation Time: 45 minutes
Cooking Time: 1 hour

Ingredients
¾ cup butter, softened
12 sheets phyllo dough

For thickener
1 cup semolina flour
3 ½ tablespoons cornstarch
1 cup white sugar
¼ teaspoon salt

For custard
6 cups whole milk

6 eggs
½ cup white sugar
1 teaspoon vanilla extract

For syrup
1 cup water
1 cup white sugar

Directions
1. In a bowl, combine the thickener ingredients. Sift or use a whisk or wooden spoon to break up any lumps. Set aside.
2. In a saucepan, bring the milk to a low boil over medium heat.
3. Gradually add the thickener ingredients to the boiling milk, stirring continuously.
4. Continue stirring with a wooden spoon until thickened and bubbling.
5. Remove from heat and set aside.
6. Using an electric mixer, beat the eggs at high speed.
7. Add the ½ cup of sugar and continue mixing until the mixture turns pale yellow (about 10 minutes)
8. Stir in the vanilla.
9. Fold the egg mixture into the hot milk mixture to make a custard. Cover partially and set it aside to cool.
10. Preheat the oven to 350°F.
11. Butter a 9x13 baking dish, and layer 7 sheets of phyllo into the pan, brushing each one with butter as you lay it in.

12. Pour the custard into the pan over the phyllo, and cover with the remaining 5 sheets of phyllo, brushing each sheet with butter as you lay it down.
13. Bake until the top crust is crisp and the custard filling has set (40 to 45 minutes).
14. To make a syrup, stir together 1 cup sugar and 1 cup of water in a small saucepan. Bring it to a boil.
15. After taking the Galaktoboureko out of the oven, spoon the hot sugar syrup over the top, particularly the edges.
16. Allow it to cool completely before cutting. Keep refrigerated.

Conclusion

Cooking dishes at home may be inconvenient but always worth it, health- and taste-wise. Some recipes are easy, while others are a little more difficult. Being in control of the quality of ingredients that you use and the amount of sodium or fat in the recipe gives you the upper hand in your diet. If you simply enjoy cooking, preparing Greek food is rewarding in itself.

Enjoy the exciting combination of flavors and colors of Greek takeout recipes!

Image Credits

Loukaniko sausages

Nikchick from Seattle, USA - Loukaniko LemonatoUploaded by Diádoco, CC BY-SA 2.0, https://commons.wikimedia.org/w/index.php?curid=10008130

Gigantes Plaki

Hevesli - Own work, Public Domain, https://commons.wikimedia.org/w/index.php?curid=5871493

Galaktoboureko

Badseed - Own work, CC BY 3.0, https://commons.wikimedia.org/w/index.php?curid=3161404

Also from Lina Chang

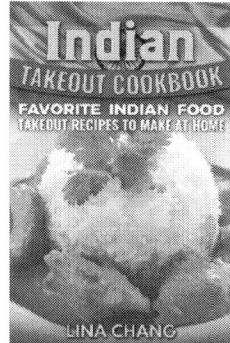

Appendix
Cooking Conversion Charts

1. Volumes

US Fluid Oz.	US	US Dry Oz.	Metric Liquid ml
¼ oz.	2 tsp.	1 oz.	10 ml.
½ oz.	1 tbsp.	2 oz.	15 ml.
1 oz.	2 tbsp.	3 oz.	30 ml.
2 oz.	¼ cup	3½ oz.	60 ml.
4 oz.	½ cup	4 oz.	125 ml.
6 oz.	¾ cup	6 oz.	175 ml.
8 oz.	1 cup	8 oz.	250 ml.

Tsp.= teaspoon - tbsp.= tablespoon – oz.= ounce – ml.= millimeter

2. Oven Temperatures

Celsius (°C)	Fahrenheit (°F)
90	220
110	225
120	250
140	275
150	300
160	325
180	350
190	375
200	400
215	425
230	450
250	475
260	500

Printed in Great Britain
by Amazon